Julie Brooke

Contents

Introduction

There are few foods that are so easy to make, that have so many wonderful varieties, that take so little time to cook than the humble waffle. This book contains 50 of the best waffle recipes– sweet and savory – that can be made with minimal effort for any meal for maximum taste and flavour. If you are looking for the ultimate collection of filling and delicious recipes for you and the family for any time of day, then this book is perfect for you.

The waffle and the waffle iron have been with us for centuries in various forms. There are few household implements that have managed to find their way into so many family homes and hearts. For ease of creation with limited time available, the waffle and all its many variations reigns supreme in the kitchen.

If you are looking for something a little different for breakfast, if you are looking for a change and some variety each day, then the waffle iron will come to your rescue every time. The waffle iron can be used for every kind of meal. As well as sweet breakfasts, it is perfect for a wide range of savory waffles for every occasion.

Waffling has been around for hundreds of years but with the modern waffle iron it has never been easier to create beautiful, warming, delicious waffles that will delight you and your family time after time.

Read on now to learn more about how to make the best waffles, the top tips and equipment and of course, the 50 best waffle recipes you will find all in one collection.

Equipment

The following are important pieces of equipment that will prove invaluable in your waffle-making. You probably have all of them anyway, but it's worth going over a couple of details first.

The Waffle Iron

The most crucial component is of course the waffle iron itself. Chances are, you are already have a waffle iron at home right now. If not, perhaps you can borrow one from a friend or family member. If you have to buy one, they can normally be found fairly cheaply at any retailer or you might be able to pick one up second hand. There are two main types of waffle iron. The circular waffle Belgian waffle iron and the more rectangular shaped iron. Either type is fine for the recipes in this book.

Many waffle irons will contain setting such as degree or browning and temperature. These can be adjusted to give you the variations of waffle ranging from soft to very crispy for example. In addition, you may see lights that indicate it is ready to bake and that the correct cooking time has elapsed. Without these however, aim to get the waffles a lovely golden-brown color before removing them.

The time taken will depend on the consistency of the batter, how much is used, the type of ingredients and other factors, but as a rough guide 5 minutes is a good start. As you get to know your waffle iron better, you will become more adept at judging the perfect baking time for your own waffles.

Always ensure your waffle iron is pre-heated before use or your timings will be out due to the time taken to reach the correct temperature. You may find it best to use a little cooking spray or oil or butter on the waffle iron itself, even if it does claim to be non-stick, before you start to ensure none of the batter sticks. The first couple of waffles in a batch may suffer this fate before the right temperature is reached or the right amount of spray is used. Experience will gradually eliminate any wastage at all.

Racks

The waffles are going to come out of the iron at a high temperature. Certain ingredients will heat up to a very high temperature inside the waffle so it's prudent to allow just a little time for the waffles to cool. Having a convenient rack nearby will allow the cooling process to be as efficient as possible.

Spatula

You will need a device to extract waffles on occasion from the iron should they stick or be left in too long and burn. A flexible spatula is ideal. Avoid any kind of metal contact that may scratch the non-stick surface.

Cloths

Always ensure you clean the waffle iron spotlessly before putting it away. Ensure the waffle iron has completely cooled down before attempting any cleaning. Leftover food and crumbs in the crevices of the iron are unhygienic and will affect the durability and lifespan of the waffle iron as well. Be meticulous about getting any remnants of food from the deepest corners of the waffle iron.

You may also find your waffle iron causes the contents of the waffle to spill out on the kitchen counter surface especially if a little too much batter has been used. Adding paper underneath the waffle which you can dispose of immediately may make life easier here.

Ingredients

One of the many great things about making waffles is the ease of producing them. They take very little time to prepare and not much longer to cook. One of the principal reasons for this is the simplicity of the ingredients used. The chances are you already have most, if not all, of the ingredients listed in this book. There might be the odd exception, but the vast majority of the recipes in this book do not call for rare or expensive or hard to find ingredients. Chances are your cupboards currently have all you need to save you time and money. Here are just a few general points about the ingredients used in the rest of the book.

Butter – assume when the recipes talk about butter, that it is unsalted.

Baking powder – this is used to lighten the waffles and is known as a leavening agent. Used instead of yeast, it's required for most of the recipes. You can test for freshness by mixing a teaspoon with a little hot water. If it produces bubbles, it's still fresh and fine to use.

Salt – Table? Kosher? Sea salt? There are various types of salt ranging from the finer table salt, to the larger flaked kosher salt to sea salt which is the least processed of the three. Use whichever you are accustomed to and feel free to experiment as you see fit.

Milk – This comes down to personal choice, but I like to opt for whole milk as I find it more flavorsome. Of course, you can go for a lower-fat milk instead if you prefer.

Eggs – Virtually all of the recipes call for eggs. In all cases where mentioned, these should be assumed to be large.

Flour – I've stuck to all-purpose flour for these recipes. Feel free to experiment a little of course with other variations if they are family favorites. I tend to go for unbleached all-purpose, but bleached will work fine as well.

Sugar – This can be altered to personal taste both in terms of color and quantity depending on how sweet you would like the waffles to be. Where mentioned however, it is assumed to be white sugar if not specified.

Top 5 Waffle Making Tips

The following tips are all designed to make the whole experience of creating and eating a wonderful waffle meal the best it can be for you and everyone eating.

1.) Ensure you can all eat at the same time. A simple one, but easy to overlook. I like to get all the waffles together, especially for a large group, so we can eat together. So they are all the same temperature, think about keeping the earliest cooked waffles in a pre-heated oven while you get the whole batch done.

2.) Read the manual! It's mentioned above, but getting to know your waffle iron is an integral part of cooking fine waffles. Use all the features available to you. Get to know the waffle iron and its intricacies and you will see better and better waffles. Always maintain and clean it afterwards.

3.) Timing is important. If you're continually lifting the lid to check on progress, you're going to find it very hard to make a perfect waffle. If you don't have a timer, then be sure to look at the steam. If it's not steaming any longer, then it's ready.

4.) Avoid the stuck waffle. Opening a waffle iron to find it ripped in two is both disappointing and time consuming to clean. Preserving your non-stick surface is a good step but if you find yourself continually cleaning up then add more oil or spray to the surface and to the recipe to eliminate the problem.

5.) Experiment. Be adventurous. If you like certain toppings more, then add them. If you like extra vanilla for example, then add another teaspoon and see how it affects the flavour. If you prefer buttermilk, then opt for that instead of milk. A waffle recipe is quite forgiving and can be seen as a guideline as much as a rigid set of instructions that have to be followed absolutely precisely.

Experimenting and bringing your own ideas and thoughts to the waffle iron to create unique family favorites is a joy. There are all sorts of foods and treats that will benefit from being waffled – don't be afraid to try them!

I know you will enjoy the great range waffle recipes in the book and are eager to get started. Without further delay, let's get waffling!

Free Gift

I would love to send you an entirely free gift – my Top 100 Cupcake Recipes. This is a whole book dedicated to the wonderful world of cupcakes and contains 100 fantastic, easy to make recipes. If you would like to get a free copy, then just follow the link below and I'll get it out to you straightaway!

Just visit here - http://eepurl.com/bWd-XL - for a free copy of the Top 100 Cupcake Recipes!

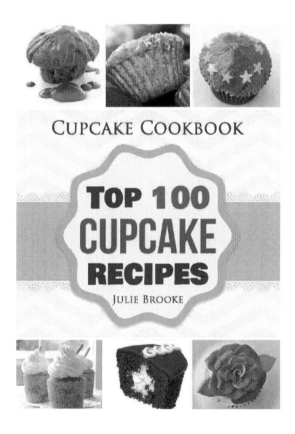

Almond Cherry Waffles

Ingredients

1 ½ cups all-purpose flour

½ cup almond meal

3 teaspoons baking powder

2 tablespoons sugar

½ teaspoon salt

1 ½ cups milk

3 eggs

2 cups pitted cherries

1 teaspoon vanilla

½ teaspoon almond extract

Directions

Preheat waffle iron. Add the flour, almond meal, sugar, baking powder and salt to a large bowl and set to one side. In a separate bowl, add the milk, eggs, vanilla and almond extract and mix. Add the wet ingredients to the dry and mix again. Fold in the 2 cups of cherries.

Add around ½ cup of batter to the waffle iron and cook for 5 minutes or until golden brown.

Apple Waffles

Ingredients

1 cup all-purpose flour

½ teaspoon salt

2 teaspoons cinnamon

2 teaspoons baking powder

½ tablespoon sugar

2 eggs

1 cup milk

3 tablespoons butter

1 cup diced apple

Directions

Using a large mixing bowl, sift together the salt, flour, cinnamon, sugar and baking powder. In a separate bowl, add the eggs, milk and butter together and mix. Add the milk mixture to the dry bowl followed by the diced apple and beat together

Once the waffle iron is preheated, add in the desired amount. Shut the lid and cook until golden brown. Remove to serve with maple syrup or a topping of fresh fruit.

Avocado and Bacon Waffles

Ingredients

2 cups all-purpose flour

2 large avocadoes, mashed

4 slices bacon

1½ cups sugar

3 teaspoons baking powder

½ teaspoon salt

1 cup milk

3 eggs

½ cup melted butter

Directions

Preheat waffle iron. Fry the bacon until very crispy. Remove from heat and crumble into a bowl. Set to one side. Add the flour, sugar, baking powder and salt into a bowl and mix together. In a separate bowl, add in the milk, melted butter, eggs and mashed avocado and whisk together. Add the wet ingredients to the dry.

Add around ½ cup to the preheated waffle iron. Sprinkle some bacon on top of the mixture and cook until golden brown. Remove and serve with any remaining avocado or bacon on the side or fresh fruit.

Bacon Waffles

Ingredients

4 slices of bacon

1 cup all-purpose flour

½ tablespoon sugar

1 teaspoon baking powder

½ teaspoon salt

1 cup milk

1 tablespoon melted butter

1 egg

Directions

Preheat waffle iron. Fry the bacon until very crispy, remove from the heat and when cooled, crumble into small pieces. Add the flour, baking powder, salt and sugar into a bowl and mix together. In a separate bowl, add the butter, eggs and milk and mix together. Add the wet ingredients to the dry and mix together.

Add a couple of tablespoons of mixture to the waffle iron and crumbled bacon on top. Cook until golden brown and serve with maple syrup for a delicious bacon breakfast.

Banana Waffles

Ingredients

1 ½ cups all-purpose flour

2 bananas, mashed

½ teaspoon salt

3 teaspoons baking powder

1 egg

1 cup milk

1 teaspoon cinnamon

½ teaspoon nutmeg

Directions

Sift in the baking powder, salt, flour, nutmeg and cinnamon into a bowl. Add in the eggs, milk and mashed banana mix together.

Once the waffle iron is preheated, spoon in the desired amount. Cook until golden, remove and serve with cream or fruit of your choice.

Beer Waffles

Ingredients

2 cups all-purpose flour

1 can beer (12 ounce)

3 teaspoons baking powder

1 teaspoon salt

½ cup milk

2 eggs

½ cup melted butter

1 ½ tablespoons honey

1 teaspoon vanilla

Directions

Preheat waffle iron. Add the flour, sugar, baking powder, and salt into a bowl and mix together. In a separate bowl, add in the milk, beer, melted butter, honey, vanilla and eggs and whisk together. Add the wet ingredients to the dry and whisk together

Add around ½ cup to the preheated waffle iron and cook until golden brown. Remove and serve with fresh fruit and maple syrup or whipped cream.

Blueberry Waffles

Ingredients

2 cups all-purpose flour

1 ½ cups blueberries

¾ teaspoon salt

1 ½ tablespoons white sugar

3 teaspoons baking powder

2 eggs

1 ½ cups milk or buttermilk

½ cup melted butter

2 teaspoons vanilla extract

Directions

Add the flour, salt, sugar and baking powder into a bowl and mix together. Add the milk, eggs, butter and vanilla into another bowl and mix. Add the contents of this bowl to the dry bowl and add in the blueberries.

Once the waffle iron is preheated, add in the desired amount. Shut the lid until cooked and remove to serve with maple syrup or a topping of fresh fruit.

Brownie Waffles

Ingredients

1 ½ cups all-purpose flour

3 tablespoons cocoa powder

½ teaspoon salt

8 ounces semisweet chocolate chips

4 tablespoons butter

1 cup sugar

3 eggs

Directions

Preheat waffle iron. Add the flour, cocoa powder and salt into a bowl and mix together. Melt the chocolate chips and butter together either in a glass bowl above a pan of boiling water or in the microwave. Take off the heat, allow to cool and add the sugar and eggs. Stir together. Add the flour mixture into the chocolate mixture and stir again.

Add the desired amount to the waffle iron and cook for about 5 minutes so it is crispy on the outside. Remove and serve with ice cream and a chopped fruit of your choice. Any type of berry goes beautifully with this dessert.

Butterscotch Waffle

Ingredients

1 ½ cups all-purpose flour

3 eggs

2 teaspoons baking powder

½ teaspoon salt

2 tablespoons sugar

4 tablespoons butter

½ teaspoon vanilla

1 ½ cups milk

½ cup butterscotch chips

Directions

Preheat waffle iron. Add the flour, baking powder, salt and sugar into a large bowl and set aside. In a separate bowl, add the butter, vanilla, eggs and milk and combine. Add the wet ingredients to the dry and mix. Fold in the butterscotch chips.

Add about ½ a cup to the waffle iron, shut the lid and cook until golden brown. Serve with whipped cream or ice cream and fruit.

Caramel Banana Waffles

Ingredients

2 cups all-purpose flour

1½ cups sugar

2 teaspoons baking powder

½ teaspoon salt

1 cup milk

3 eggs

½ cup melted butter

2 chopped bananas

Sauce

1 cup brown sugar

½ cup water

½ cup melted butter

¼ cup milk

1 teaspoons vanilla

Directions

Preheat waffle iron. Add the flour, sugar, baking powder, and salt into a bowl and mix together. In a separate bowl, add in the milk, melted butter and eggs and whisk together. Add the wet ingredients to the dry and combine.

To make the sauce, boil the sugar, butter and milk slowly until the desired thickness is reached. Allow to cool slightly and add the vanilla.

Add around ½ cup of the batter to the preheated waffle iron and cook until golden brown. Serve with the chopped bananas and hot caramel sauce poured on the top.

Cheese and Sausage Waffles

Ingredients

2 cups all-purpose flour

¾ pound sausage (any type you like)

½ cup grated sharp Cheddar

3 teaspoons baking powder

½ teaspoon salt

1 cup milk

3 eggs

½ cup melted butter

Directions

Preheat waffle iron. Cook the sausages, remove from heat and cut into small slices. Add the flour, baking powder and salt into a bowl and combine. In a separate bowl, add the eggs, milk and butter and mix. Add the wet ingredients to the dry. Now fold in the cheese and sausage slices.

Add about ½ a cup of batter to the waffle iron and cook until golden brown. Remove from heat and serve with maple syrup.

Chocolate Waffles

Ingredients

2 cups all-purpose flour

½ cup sugar

1 tablespoon baking powder

1 tablespoon cocoa powder

½ teaspoons salt

1 cup butter

1 ½ cups semi-sweet chocolate chips

1 ½ cups milk

3 eggs

1 tablespoon vanilla

Directions

Preheat the waffle iron. Add the flour, sugar, cocoa powder, baking powder and salt into a bowl and mix together. Melt the butter and chocolate chips together using either a microwave or a glass bowl over a saucepan of boiling water. Remove to cool a little. Add in the milk, eggs and vanilla and stir. Add this mixture to the dry bowl ingredients and mix together.

Add the mixture to the waffle iron and cook. Serve hot with cream or ice-cream on the top.

Cinnamon Waffles

Ingredients

1 cups all-purpose flour

2 eggs

1 cup milk

¼ cup melted butter

2 teaspoons baking powder

½ teaspoon baking soda

1 tablespoon sugar

¼ teaspoon salt

1 teaspoon cinnamon

Directions

Add the eggs, vanilla, egg and butter into a bowl and mix together. In a separate bowl, add the flour, cinnamon, baking powder, baking soda, salt and sugar and mix. Combine the wet ingredients with the dry.

Add the mixture onto your preheated waffle iron. Shut the lid until cooked and remove to serve with maple syrup, whipped cream or a topping of fresh fruit.

Cornbread Waffles

Ingredients

1 cup cornmeal (yellow)

½ cup all-purpose flour

1 ½ teaspoons baking powder

½ teaspoon baking soda

½ teaspoon salt

1 cup milk

½ cup melted butter

1 egg

2 tablespoons sugar

Directions

Preheat waffle iron. Add the cornmeal, baking powder, salt, baking soda into a large bowl and mix. In another bowl, add the milk, butter and egg. Add the wet ingredients to the dry and stir.

Add about ½ cup of the mixture to the waffle iron and cook until golden brown.

Dark Chocolate Waffles

Ingredients

2 cups all-purpose flour

½ cup cocoa powder, unsweetened

½ cup brown sugar

2 teaspoons baking powder

½ teaspoon salt

4 tablespoons butter

2 cups milk

3 eggs

1 teaspoon vanilla

1 cup dark chocolate chips

Directions

Preheat waffle iron. Add the flour, cocoa powder, sugar, baking powder and salt into a large bowl and set aside. In a separate bowl, add the eggs, milk, butter and vanilla and beat together. Add the wet ingredients to the dry and mix together. Fold in the chocolate chips.

Add around ½ cup of batter and cook for about 5 minutes. Serve with ice cream on the side or if you are feeling particularly, decadent, melt some additional chocolate and pour over the top of the hot waffles for a real treat.

Egg Nog Waffles

These make a wonderful seasonal treat and are quick and easy to make for guests or just for yourself!

Ingredients

2 cups all-purpose flour

1 tablespoon sugar

3 teaspoons baking powder

1 teaspoon salt

¾ teaspoon cinnamon

½ teaspoon nutmeg

2 cups eggnog

1 tablespoon butter

2 eggs

Directions

Preheat waffle iron. Add the flour, baking powder, sugar, salt, cinnamon and nutmeg into a bowl and combine together. In a separate bowl, add the eggnog, eggs and butter and mix. Add the wet ingredients to the dry.

Add around ½ cup of batter to the waffle iron, close and cook until golden brown. Serve hot.

French Toast Waffles

These are easy to make. Just make sure the bread is thick (about half an inch) and reasonably hard otherwise it will collapse easily.

Ingredients

Thick bread slices

2 eggs

½ cup milk

½ teaspoon cinnamon

1 teaspoon vanilla

1 tablespoon butter

1 tablespoon sugar

Directions

Preheat waffle iron and spray to ensure nothing sticks. Add the eggs, milk, sugar, vanilla, butter and cinnamon into a large bowl and mix together. Dip the bread into the mixture so it is well coated on both sides. Add to the waffle iron and cook for about 3 minutes or until golden brown. Serve with a little dusting of sugar on top.

Glazed Donut Waffles

Ingredients

2 cups all-purpose flour

3 eggs

4 tablespoons butter

½ cup sugar

2 teaspoons baking powder

1 teaspoon vanilla

Glaze

2 cups confectioners' sugar

1 cup milk

1 teaspoon vanilla

Chocolate chips (optional)

Sprinkles (optional)

Directions

Preheat waffle iron. Add the flour, baking powder and sugar to a bowl and set aside. In a separate bowl, add the milk, eggs, butter and vanilla extract and mix together. Add the wet ingredients to the dry and mix.

For the glaze, add the ingredients to a bowl and mix together. You can change the consistency by adding more milk or more confectioners' sugar. Add around ½ cup of batter to the waffle iron and cook until golden brown. Remove from the waffle iron and dunk in the glaze. Add in chocolate chips or sprinkles or whatever topping takes your fancy to serve!

Grilled Cheese Waffles

You can make a grilled cheese a number of ways, but using a waffle iron lends it a certain unique look and crunch that is unbeatable. Adapt this recipe for your own favorite cheeses, but once you've tried it, you won't go back to making them any other way.

Ingredients

4 slices of bread

Butter

Cheddar

Directions

Preheat waffle iron. Butter both sides of the bread to prevent it sticking. Add the cheese into the middle and place on the waffle iron. Shut it, but be sure to check after 2 or 3 minutes to ensure it hasn't gone past golden brown.

Remove (be careful of cheese spilling through) and serve hot. Add tomato or your favorite sandwich meat for variety next time.

Hash Brown and Cheese Waffle

Ingredients

1 bag (30 ounce) shredded hash browns

1 teaspoon salt

1 cup Cheddar

3 eggs

¼ cup milk

Pinch of pepper

1 cup diced ham

Directions

Preheat waffle iron. Add the hash browns, ham, cheese, eggs, milk, salt and pepper to a large bowl and mix together. Add about ½ a cup to the heated waffle iron, shut the lid and cook for about 4 to 5 minutes or until golden brown.

Honey Waffles

These ooze honey flavour as you eat them and taste delicious.
Serve with fresh bananas for an energy-packed start to the day.

Ingredients

2 cups all-purpose flour

1 ½ tablespoons sugar

3 tablespoons butter, melted

3 eggs

3 tablespoons honey

3 teaspoons baking powder

½ teaspoon salt

1 teaspoon cinnamon

1 ½ cups milk

Directions

Preheat waffle iron. Add the flour, sugar, baking powder,
cinnamon and salt to a large bowl and set aside. In a different bowl,
add the eggs, milk, butter and honey and combine. Add the wet
ingredients to the dry and mix.

Add about ½ cup of batter to the waffle iron, shut the lid and cook
for 5 minutes or until golden brown. Serve hot.

Jam Waffles

I've not specified the type of jam you can use here – pretty much anything goes. Try it with your favorite for a delicious breakfast every time.

Ingredients

2 cups all-purpose flour

½ teaspoon salt

1 ½ tablespoons white sugar

3 teaspoons baking powder

3 eggs

1 cup milk

½ cup melted butter

Jam – your favorite

Directions

Preheat the waffle iron. Add the flour, salt, sugar and baking powder into a bowl and mix together. In a separate bowl, add the eggs milk and butter and whisk together. Add the wet ingredients to the dry and mix.

Add around ¼ cup of batter to the waffle iron. As this starts to cook, add some jam on to the center, followed by another ¼ cup of batter. Shut the waffle iron and cook for a couple of minutes. Remove to serve. Ideal with ice cream on top.

Lemon Waffles

Ingredients

2 cups all-purpose flour

1 cup of lemon zest

1 tablespoon lemon juice

1½ cups sugar

2 teaspoons baking powder

½ teaspoon salt

1 cup milk

3 eggs

½ cup melted butter

Directions

Preheat waffle iron. Add the flour, sugar, baking powder, and salt into a bowl and mix together. Add in the lemon zest and stir again. In a separate bowl, add in the milk, lemon juice, melted butter and eggs and whisk together. Add the wet ingredients to the dry.

Add around ½ cup to the preheated waffle iron and cook until golden brown. Remove and serve with any fresh fruit and maple syrup.

Mango Waffles

Ingredients

2 cups all-purpose flour

1 mango, diced

1½ cups sugar

3 teaspoons baking powder

½ teaspoon salt

½ teaspoon nutmeg

1 teaspoon vanilla

1 cup milk

3 eggs

½ cup melted butter

Directions

Preheat waffle iron. Add the flour, sugar, baking powder, nutmeg and salt into a bowl and mix together. In a separate bowl, add in the milk, melted butter, vanilla and eggs and whisk together. Add the wet ingredients to the dry. Fold in the diced mango.

Add around ½ cup to the preheated waffle iron and cook until golden brown. Remove and serve with any remaining mango on top, drizzled with honey.

Mint Chocolate Waffles

Ingredients

2 cups all-purpose flour

1 cup sugar

1 tablespoon baking powder

½ cup cocoa powder, unsweetened

½ teaspoons salt

1 cup butter

1 teaspoon mint extract

1 cup semi-sweet chocolate chips

1 ½ cups milk

3 eggs

Directions

Preheat waffle iron. Add the flour, cocoa powder, baking powder, salt and sugar to a bowl. In a separate bowl, add the butter, mint extract, eggs and milk and combine. Add the wet ingredients to the dry and mix together. Fold in the chocolate chips.

Add about ½ cup of batter to the waffle iron and cook for around 5 minutes. Remove from heat and cover with a little confectioners' sugar or whipped cream or vanilla ice-cream on the side.

Mocha Waffles

Waffles and coffee go together like a dream, so it makes sense a mocha waffle would be the perfect accompaniment to a strong cup of coffee. Try this recipe for a great start to any day.

Ingredients

2 cups all-purpose flour

3 tablespoons butter, melted

½ cup coffee

3 teaspoons baking powder

½ teaspoon salt

½ cup cocoa, unsweetened

½ cup brown sugar

2 tablespoons espresso powder

3 eggs

2 cups milk

½ cup semi-sweet chocolate chips(optional)

Directions

Preheat waffle iron. Add the coffee and butter into a pan and melt together. Set to one side. Add the flour, baking powder, salt, cocoa, sugar and espresso into a bowl and set aside. In a separate bowl, add the milk and eggs and mix together. Add the milk, along the with melted butter mix into the dry ingredients and combine. If you've gone for the chocolate chips, then fold these in now.

Add about ½ cup of batter to the waffle iron, shut the lid and cook for 5 minutes. Remove from heat and sprinkle with a little confectioners' sugar on top.

Nutella Waffles

Ingredients

2 cups all-purpose flour

1 teaspoon salt

2 teaspoons baking powder

4 tablespoons Nutella

1/3 cup chopped almonds (optional)

2 eggs

1 ½ cups milk or buttermilk

2 teaspoons vanilla extract

Directions

Add the flour, salt, chopped almonds and baking powder to a bowl and mix together. Beat the eggs in a separate bowl and add the milk and vanilla extract. Add the contents of the wet bowl to the dry, followed by the Nutella and mix together. Add the milk and combine.

Add the desired amount to the pre-heated waffle iron. Once cooked, serve with fresh fruit or maple syrup.

Oatmeal Waffles

These are perfect for a tasty and filling breakfast.

Ingredients

2 cups all-purpose flour

1 cup oats

3 teaspoons baking powder

½ teaspoon salt

3 eggs

2 cups milk

4 tablespoons butter

2 tablespoons sugar

1 teaspoon vanilla

Directions

Add the flour, oats, salt and baking powder into a bowl and mix together. In a separate bowl, add the eggs, milk, sugar and butter and beat together. Add the wet bowl contents to the dry and mix together.

Add the desired amounts to your waffle iron and when cooked serve with fresh fruit of your choosing.

Onion Waffles

Ingredients

2 cups all-purpose flour

½ cup butter, melted

3 eggs

½ cup sugar

½ teaspoon salt

2 teaspoons baking powder

1 ½ cups milk

3 large onions, sliced

1 cup sharp Cheddar

Directions

Preheat waffle iron. Add the flour, baking powder, sugar and salt into a bowl and set aside. Add the sliced onions to a skillet and cook in a little butter until tender. In a separate bowl, add the butter, eggs and milk and whisk together. Add the wet ingredients to the dry and mix. Fold in the cooked onions and the cheese and mix together.

Add around ½ cup of batter to the waffle iron, close and cook until golden brown. Serve hot with a little salt.

Orange Waffles

The orange flavor lends a lovely freshness to these waffles. Try them once and you won't be disappointed.

Ingredients

2 cups all-purpose flour

$\frac{1}{2}$ teaspoon salt

1 tablespoon white sugar

3 teaspoons baking powder

3 eggs

$\frac{1}{2}$ cup milk

$\frac{3}{4}$ cup orange juice

3 tablespoons orange zest

4 tablespoons melted butter

Directions

Add the baking powder, sugar, flour and salt into a bowl and mix. Take another bowl and add in the eggs, orange juice, milk and butter. Beat together and add in the zest of the oranges. Add everything to the flour bowl and beat together lightly.

Add the mixture in the desired quantities to the waffle iron. You can serve with fruit or maple syrup or simply dust with sugar.

Peach Waffles

Ingredients

2 cups all-purpose flour

½ cup butter

3 eggs

½ cup sugar

2 teaspoons baking powder

1 ½ cups milk

2 cups diced peaches

1 teaspoon vanilla

½ teaspoon cinnamon

Directions

Preheat waffle iron. Add the butter, sugar and eggs into a large bowl and beat together. Add in the flour, baking powders, salt and cinnamon into a separate bowl and mix together. Add the dry ingredients to the wet, followed by the milk and vanilla. Finally, add the diced peaches.

Add the desired amount to the preheated waffle iron and cook until golden brown. Remove and serve with syrup, fresh cream or ice cream.

Peanut Butter Waffles

Ingredients

1 ½ cups all-purpose flour

½ teaspoon salt

2 ½ tablespoons white sugar

1 tablespoon baking powder

2 eggs

1 ½ cups milk or buttermilk

½ cup melted butter

½ cup peanut butter

Directions

Add the flour, baking powder, salt and sugar into a bowl and combine together. In a separate bowl, add the milk, eggs, peanut butter and butter and beat. Add the milk bowl contents into the dry bowl and mix together.

Add the desired amount to the waffle iron. Remove to a warm plate and serve with maple syrup or your favorite jelly flavor.

Peanut Butter Waffles

Ingredients

2 cups all-purpose flour

½ cup creamy peanut butter

2 eggs

2 cups milk

½ cup melted butter

3 teaspoons baking powder

½ teaspoon salt

3 tablespoons sugar

Directions

Preheat waffle iron. Add the flour, sugar, baking powder and salt into a bowl and mix together. Add in the peanut butter, butter, eggs and milk into a separate bowl and mix together. Add the peanut butter mix to the flour bowl and stir together.

Add around ½ cup to the preheated waffle iron and cook until golden brown. Remove and serve with syrup, fresh cream or ice cream.

Pear Waffles

Ingredients

2 cups all-purpose flour

1½ cups sugar

3 teaspoons baking powder

½ teaspoon salt

2 cups milk

3 eggs

½ cup melted butter

2 diced pears

Directions

Preheat waffle iron. Add the flour, sugar, baking powder and salt into a bowl and mix together. In a separate bowl, add in the milk, melted butter and eggs and whisk together. Add the wet ingredients to the dry. Fold in the pears.

Add around ½ cup to the preheated waffle iron and cook until golden brown. Remove and serve with syrup, fresh cream or ice cream.

Pecan Waffles

Ingredients

2 cups all-purpose flour

½ cup butter

2 eggs

½ teaspoon salt

2 teaspoons baking powder

1 cup pecans

2 cups milk

Directions

Preheat waffle iron. Heat the oven to 300 degrees and add the pecans to a sheet. Toast in the oven for about 8 minutes. Remove and when cooled, chop into small pieces and set aside. In a bowl, add together the flour, baking powder and salt. In a separate bowl and the eggs and milk and whisk together. Add the wet ingredients to the dry. Fold in the chopped pecans.

Add the desired amount onto the waffle iron and cook until golden brown. Remove and serve hot with maple syrup.

Pecan Waffles

Ingredients

2 cups all-purpose flour

1 cup pecans, chopped

3 teaspoons baking powder

½ teaspoon salt

1 cup milk

3 eggs

½ cup melted butter

Directions

Preheat waffle iron. Add the flour, sugar, baking powder, and salt into a bowl and mix together. In a separate bowl, add in the milk, melted butter and eggs and whisk together. Add the wet ingredients to the dry and mix. Fold in the chopped pecans.

Add around ½ cup to the preheated waffle iron and cook until golden brown. Remove and serve with any fresh fruit and maple syrup.

Pineapple Waffles

Ingredients

1 ½ cups all-purpose flour

2 tablespoons sugar

1 can crushed pineapple

1 cup milk

3 eggs

4 tablespoons butter

2 teaspoons baking powder

½ teaspoon salt

Directions

Preheat waffle iron. Add the flour, sugar, salt and baking powder into a large bowl. In a separate bowl, add the milk, eggs and butter and mix together. Add the wet ingredients to the dry and mix again. Fold in the crushed pineapple.

Add around ½ cup of batter to the waffle iron and cook until golden brown. Serve hot.

Pizza Waffles

This might sound a surprising combination, but they're so easy to make, take no time and taste wonderful.

Ingredients

1 can biscuit dough

1 ½ cups mozzarella

Pepperoni

Pizza sauce

Directions

Preheat waffle iron. Flatten out each biscuit to about a 6-inch diameter. Add on the pizza sauce, followed by a slice of mozzarella, then as much pepperoni as you like. Add another slice of cheese on top. Take another biscuit and flatten it out to a 6-inch diameter again. Cover one side in pizza sauce and place this side face down on top of the second slice of cheese.

Shut the waffle iron and cook for about 5 minutes. Serve for a delicious and quick and easy treat.

Potato Waffles

Ingredients

1 chopped onion

1 crushed garlic clove

2 ½ cups mashed potato

¼ cup all-purpose flour

3 eggs

½ teaspoon salt

2 tablespoons grated Parmesan

Directions

Add the onion and garlic to a pan and cook for 10 minutes or until the onion is very soft. Remove from the heat. Add the mashed potato, flour, eggs, cheese and salt into a large bowl and mix together. Add the desired quantity to a preheated waffle iron and cook.

These potato waffles should emerge golden brown and make an awesome side dish to a wide variety of mains.

Pumpkin Waffles

Ingredients

2 cups all-purpose flour

3 teaspoons baking powder

3 tablespoons butter, melted

2 teaspoons cinnamon

1 teaspoon nutmeg

1 teaspoon ground ginger

½ teaspoon salt

3 eggs

2 tablespoons sugar

1 can pumpkin puree

2 cups milk

Directions

Preheat waffle iron. Add the flour, baking powder, cinnamon, salt, nutmeg and ginger into a bowl and set aside. In a separate bowl, add the eggs, milk, sugar, puree and butter and combine. Add the wet ingredients to the dry ingredients and mix.

Add around ½ cup of batter to the waffle iron, close and cook until golden brown. Serve hot with maple syrup.

Raspberry Waffles

Ingredients

2 cups all-purpose flour

1 ½ cups raspberries (frozen and defrosted or fresh)

¾ teaspoon salt

1 ½ tablespoons white sugar

3 teaspoons baking powder

2 eggs

1 ½ cups milk or buttermilk

½ cup melted butter

2 teaspoons vanilla extract

Directions

Add the flour, salt, sugar and baking powder into a bowl and mix together. Add the milk, eggs, butter and vanilla into another bowl and mix. Add the wet ingredients to the dry and fold in the raspberries.

Once the waffle iron is preheated, add in the desired amount. Shut the lid until cooked and remove to serve with maple syrup or a topping of sugar and fruit.

Red Velvet Glazed Waffle

These look beautiful and are perfect for a romantic breakfast – give them a try yourself today!

Ingredients

2 cups all-purpose flour

½ cup sugar

4 teaspoons baking powder

½ teaspoon salt

2 cups milk

4 tablespoons melted butter

1 tablespoon cocoa powder

2 eggs

2 teaspoons vanilla

½ teaspoon white vinegar

2 ½ tablespoons red food coloring

Glaze

6 ounces cream cheese

6 tablespoons butter

1 ½ cups confectioners' sugar

2 teaspoons vanilla

½ - ¾ cup milk

Directions

Preheat the waffle iron and start on the glaze first. Add the cream cheese and butter into a bowl and beat together. Slowly add in the sugar while continuing to whisk, followed by the milk and vanilla. If a little thick, then add some more milk. Set aside for later.

For the waffles, add the flour, cocoa powder, baking powder and sugar into a bowl. In a different bowl, add in the milk, butter, vanilla, eggs and vinegar and beat together. Add in the food coloring. Add the wet ingredients to the dry and whisk. Add about a cup of the mixture onto the waffle iron and allow to cook. The waffle should be crisp with a velvet color. Remove to serve hot with the glaze dripped onto the top.

Rice Waffle

If you have some leftover rice from dinner, then it will taste great the next day with this rice waffle recipe.

Ingredients

2 cups all-purpose flour

½ teaspoon salt

1 ½ tablespoons white sugar

3 teaspoons baking powder

3 eggs

1 cups milk

½ cup melted butter

1 cup cooked rice

Directions

Preheat the waffle iron. Add the flour, salt, sugar and baking powder into a bowl and mix together. In a separate bowl, add the eggs milk and butter and whisk together. Add the wet ingredients to the dry and mix. Fold in the cooked rice.

Add around ½ a cup of batter to the waffle iron and cook until golden brown.

Smoked Salmon Waffles

Ingredients

2 cups all-purpose flour

3 tablespoons butter

3 teaspoons baking powder

½ teaspoon salt

½ teaspoon ground pepper

3 cups milk

3 eggs

3 ounces smoked salmon, chopped

2 scallions, chopped

3 teaspoons dill

1 teaspoon lemon juice

Directions

Preheat waffle iron. Add the flour, baking powder, salt and pepper and set aside. In a separate bowl, add the butter, milk and eggs and combine. Add the wet ingredients to the dry and mix together. Fold in the salmon, scallions, dill and lemon juice.

Add around ½ cup of batter to the waffle iron, shut the lid and cook until golden brown. Serve hot with a little cream cheese or just additional lemon and fresh pepper.

Sour Cream Waffles

Ingredients

2 cups all-purpose flour

3 teaspoons baking powder

2 tablespoons sugar

1 cup sour cream

1 cup milk

3 tablespoons butter

3 eggs

1 teaspoon vanilla

Directions

Preheat waffle iron. Add the flour, baking powder and sugar to a bowl and set aside. In a separate bowl, add the sour cream, milk, butter, eggs and vanilla and mix. Add the wet ingredients to the dry and combine.

Add around ½ cup of batter to the waffle iron and cook for 5 minutes or until golden brown. Serve with fresh fruit.

Strawberry Waffles

Ingredients

2 cups all-purpose flour

½ cup melted butter

½ teaspoon salt

3 eggs

1 cup sugar

3 teaspoons baking powder

2 cups milk

1 ½ cups strawberries, chopped

1 teaspoon vanilla

Directions

Preheat waffle iron. Add the flour, baking powder and salt into a bowl and mix together. Using a different bowl, add the milk, butter, vanilla, eggs and sugar together and mix. Add the wet ingredients into the dry and story together. Finally, add in the chopped strawberries.

Add a little less than ½ cup to the preheated waffle iron and cook until golden brown. Remove and serve with syrup, fresh cream or ice cream.

Sweet Potato Waffle

Ingredients

2 cups sweet potato puree

1 cup milk

1 egg

2 tablespoon melted, unsalted butter

1 ½ cups all-purpose flour

2 tablespoons sugar

1 ½ tablespoons baking powder

2 teaspoons cinnamon

½ teaspoon nutmeg

½ teaspoon ginger

¼ teaspoon salt

Directions

Preheat the waffle iron. Add in the sweet potato, milk, egg and butter into a large bowl and mix together. In a different bowl, mix together the sugar, flour, baking powder, cinnamon, nutmeg, ginger and salt. Add the dry ingredients to the wet and stir together.

Spoon the mixture into the waffle iron and cook until golden brown. Remove to plate and serve hot.

The Classic Waffle

Ingredients

2 cups all-purpose flour

1/2 teaspoon salt

2 tablespoons white sugar

4 teaspoons baking powder

2 eggs

1 ½ cups milk or buttermilk

½ cup melted butter

2 teaspoons vanilla extract

Directions

Preheat the waffle iron. Add the flour, salt, baking powder and sugar into a large bowl and mix together. Using a different bowl, add the eggs and beat together. Pour in the milk, butter and vanilla and stir. Now add the liquid bowl contents into the flour bowl and beat together.

Add the mixture to your waffle iron and cook until golden. If you like the waffles a little sweeter, then add a fraction more sugar next time. Add in your favorite topping with some maple syrup for a delicious waffle meal!

White Chocolate Waffle

If you're a fan of white chocolate, then these will be a treat every time!

Ingredients

1 egg

1 cup flour

1 teaspoon baking powder

¼ teaspoon salt

½ tablespoon sugar

½ cup milk

1 tablespoon vanilla extract

4 tablespoons butter

½ cup white chocolate chips

Directions

Preheat waffle iron. Add the flour, baking powder, salt and sugar into a bowl and mix together. In a separate bowl, add the egg, milk, butter and vanilla and combine together. Pour this mixture over the dry ingredients and mix. Add in the white chips and fold in. Spoon on to the waffle iron and cook!

Yogurt Waffles

These have a lovely deep flavour to them. Top with fresh fruit of your choosing for a breakfast to set you up for the day

Ingredients

1 ½ cups all-purpose flour

2 cups vanilla yogurt

3 eggs

½ teaspoon salt

3 teaspoons baking powder

1 teaspoon vanilla

¼ cup vegetable oil

Directions

Preheat waffle iron. Add the eggs into a bowl and whisk. Follow with the yogurt, baking powder, flour, salt, oil and vanilla and mix together.

Add about ½ a cup to the waffle iron and cook for 5 minutes or until golden brown.

Zucchini Waffles

Ingredients

2 cups all-purpose flour

1 cup zucchini puree

3 eggs

2 tablespoons melted butter

1 cup oats

2 teaspoons baking powder

1 ½ tablespoons sugar

½ teaspoon salt

2 teaspoons cinnamon

Directions

Preheat waffle iron. Add the milk, zucchini, butter and eggs into a bowl and mix together. In a separate bowl, add the flour, oats, baking powder, sugar, cinnamon and salt. Add the dry ingredients to the zucchini bowl and mix.

Add the mixture to the waffle iron and cook until the waffles are golden brown.